Content

I0031966

From the Editor

Welcome to the inaugural issue of PIVOT Magazine. We're a periodical designed from the ground up for entrepreneurs and business people of all kinds.

This first issue is all about public relations and how you can use PR to grow your business faster than you ever thought possible. James Foo Torres of Imperium Authority has proven himself in the PR trenches. We first became aware of his unique skills when we saw the work he did for the Strategic Advisor Board.

PIVOT's founder and president, Jason Miller, is a business powerhouse in his own right. He owns several successful businesses he has built, scaled, and grown. He is also the CEO of the Strategic Advisor Board, a fast-growing business strategy and consulting firm.

Joel Phillips, CEO of Proshark, is the creative genius behind the PIVOT website.

Laura West is a multi-talented editor and project manager. She is also my executive assistant and has helped guide many policy decisions at JETLAUNCH.

Last, I am Chris O'Byrne, Editor-in-Chief. I am also the CEO of JETLAUNCH, one of ten directors at the Strategic Advisor Board, plus co-founder and co-director of Rogue Publishing Partners.

PIVOT Magazine

Founder and President
Jason Miller
jason@strategicadvisorboard.com

Editor-in-Chief
Chris O'Byrne
chris@jetlaunch.net

Design
JETLAUNCH.net

Advertising
Chris O'Byrne
chris@jetlaunch.net

Webmaster
Joel Phillips
joel@proshark.com

Editor
Laura West
laura@jetlaunch.net

Why Public Relations Needs to Be Part of Your Marketing Plan

James Foo Torres

Who said it is unimportant. The underlying assertion is that advertising is a crapshoot which often delivers unreliable results. Until the emergence of digital advertising, it was difficult to measure the effectiveness of print, broadcast, outdoor, and other forms of advertising. A notable exception was junk mail. Due to the nature of direct response, a marketer could know down to the penny how many recipients responded and what they ordered/spent.

Fortunately, the days of shooting in the dark and not knowing what missed the target or how much revenue responses generated are over.

Thanks to the immediacy of electronic advertising and marketing automation technology, click-throughs, conversions, and sales volume can now be tracked with a highly accurate granularity. Reviewing this data, conducting A and B testing, and continually fine-tuning marketing programs ensures that only marketers not paying attention waste any of their ad budget, let alone not know which is wasted or which is producing results.

The power of PR

By the same token, business owners and executives interested in gaining the best ROI possible are committing a similar degree of fiscal malfeasance if they don't include public relations in the mix of their marketing efforts.

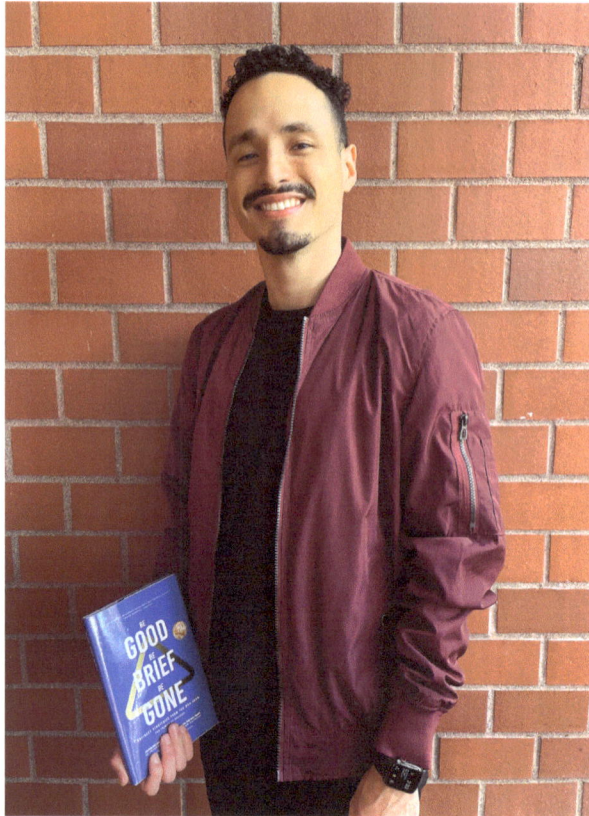

Long ago, a business executive famously said, "Half of all of the money I spend on advertising is wasted. I just don't know which half." This quote is often credited to marketing pioneer and retail magnate John Wanamaker. Others claim it was first said by William Hesketh Lever, a British industrialist who was the first to commercially turn vegetable oil into soap, the basis for the success of the Lever Brothers company, now Unilever, a $115 billion multinational.

> **Don't push people where you want them to be. Meet them where they are.**
> – Meghan Keaney Anderson,
> VP Marketing, HubSpot

You might ask, "Why should public relations be an essential element of any cost-effective and comprehensive marketing-communications plan?" The reasons are so compelling that it's perplexing that so many entrepreneurs and executives have what I call a "PR blind spot." Let's start with a definition of what public relations actually is and why it can be so powerful.

The Public Relations Society of America, the largest industry association for PR professionals, defines it as a process of "strategic communication which builds mutually beneficial relationships between organizations and their publics." What exactly does that mean and how does this process work?

In contrast to paid advertising which buys time, space or pixels on a content platform (newspaper, magazine, airwaves, website, streaming service) to transmit a message to consumers on a content platform, the process of running a PR campaign is quite different. For starters, the primary goal is to accomplish the same thing as advertising, but without paying. In other words, instead of purchasing access to an audience, public relations professionals create an incentive for the same platforms to provide editorial coverage at no cost.

That incentive takes the form of a newsworthy pitch. When it works, it can deliver hundreds of thousands or even millions of dollars of free marketing in the form of zero-cost impressions with a local, regional, or national audience. Once a business owner or marketing executive thinks of it that way, it becomes a highly compelling proposition. Afterall, why pay for something you can get for free?

Content is king.
Newsworthy content gets covered

While the successful placement of a story with a news organization might seem like alchemy to anyone unfamiliar with how news organizations function, it makes perfect sense from the perspective of

"If I was down to my last dollar, I'd spend it on public relations."

– Bill Gates

publishers and news directors. Think about it: the editors and reporters responsible for populating the 24/7 news cycle with stories and information need story ideas.

Here's how it works: the job of editors is to find newsworthy stories and assign them to reporters. The reporter (or freelancer) writes an outline for their article, interviews subject matter experts, government officials, eyewitnesses, or whomever is a logical source of information, and types the story out on a computer in the newsroom. In the case of television or radio, the same process occurs, with the exception that the story is written and then captured on video or audio.

Professionals working in the field of journalism take their jobs very seriously. Most are college or university educated. Many are exceedingly worldly and have traveled extensively. As practitioners of an honorable profession, they take pride in what they do and want to do their jobs well. There's even a Journalist's Creed which spells out the responsibilities and ethics which should be observed to ensure the public interest is well served. They were written in 1914 by Walter Williams, the founding dean of the Missouri School of Journalism and have been published in over 100 languages.

Here are a few of the eight principles it advocates:

- I believe that the public journal is a public trust; that all connected with it are, to the full measure of their responsibility, trustees for the public; that acceptance of a lesser service than the public service is betrayal of this trust.
- I believe that clear thinking and clear statements, accuracy and

fairness are fundamental to good journalism.

- I believe that a journalist should write only what he holds in his heart to be true.
- I believe that suppression of the news, for any consideration other than the welfare of society, is indefensible.

You can read the rest of the principles here.

Starting your PR program

Even those who understand the potential benefits PR could deliver to their business, often think they don't have a story interesting enough to warrant news coverage. *Why would the news media think I'm worthy of writing about?* they wonder.

There are three valid reasons why you should sit down with a PR expert and explore the possibilities. They will explain to you why PR works and why.

1. **Creating news content is expensive, so provide it to them!**

A leading daily newspaper in a major metropolitan market might have dozens or even hundreds of employees in the newsroom. Editors, reporters, news desk managers and other contributors can cost millions annually in payroll. Due to the emergence of the Internet, the way people get their local and national news has

changed radically. Every newspaper in the world has experienced a precipitous drop in their subscriber base, resulting in layoffs and a reliance on freelance reporters and writers. Therefore, smaller staffs mean a bigger reliance on story ideas and content from public relations agencies.

2. Interesting news stories drive readership

The fact is, publishers need content! If your in-house publicist or public relations agency can provide high quality, newsworthy stories about your business, it will likely be reviewed for potential assignment to a reporter. To make the pitch even more compelling, consider offering your news item as a scoop, which means you're only making it available to the chosen news outlet as an exclusive. Beating competing news organizations is a competitive advantage and draws eyeballs. Over time, this builds the audience which in turn drives advertising revenue, the lifeblood of print, broadcast, web, and streaming news services.

3. Virtually any product, service or company has a newsworthy angle if you seek it out

There's an old expression in the newspaper industry about what is newsworthy and what is not.

A dog bites a man. That's not news. But if a man bites a dog—now that's news! The point is, even if you have the mistaken belief that your story, whether it be your personal entrepreneurial journey or the business you're building, isn't newsworthy—well, you're right if you approach PR from that perspective. On the other hand, by working with a PR pro, you'll not only uncover some compelling, newsworthy angles together which exist in your business already, you'll both come up with entirely new ideas which make your story worth covering.

For example, if you make widgets, you'd be correct to assume that few journalists would be interested in the fact that on Monday you're releasing a new model of your widget. Only a new iPhone model announcement by Apple can command the attention of news outlets around the world. How rarified is that status? Can you remember the press swooning over Nike dropping a new model of running shoe? Shoe collectors and avid sports fans might care, but the average person has too much going on in their own lives to have even a small amount of interest.

But, if you tell the press that your new widget can be used to reduce CO_2 emissions or save lives, that is a newsworthy pitch. Or, if you plan to donate some widgets to a non-profit, that might grab an editor's attention. Whatever the newsworthy angle you and your PR consultant come up with, remember these requisites:

It must be true

Deceptive or non-factual pitches fall apart quickly under scrutin y and then you've lost all credibility.

It must be interesting

Put yourself in the journalist's shoes. Is your story worth covering because it's something the average person would not be aware of up until they see the story? Is the topic unusual or offbeat? Finding the best, most compelling aspect is the job of your PR agency. That's what they do!

It must have a point

People today are busy, distracted, and often juggling several tasks at once. If they have the news on the TV or radio, it's probably background noise. When they see something on a website, their eyes will glance over the headline of an article and then scroll down or click away.

To be an attention-grabber, your story first has to gain the interest of an editor or reporter before you even get a shot at a reader or viewer.

Everyone in the media is trying to build an audience. When a news item comes along which includes a human interest angle, useful information, or something which offers 'takeaway' value, journalists take notice because it has the potential to deliver value to the public.

Convinced PR is something you simply must do from now on? Great! Here's the sequence of steps you'll be walked through by your publicist:

First, they'll want to analyze your goals

Do you want to elevate the profile of your company, position yourself as a voice of authority, raise awareness of a new product line or service, publicize a worthwhile cause which will make the world a better place? Each of these are common objectives and fully achievable if you're in the capable hands of an experienced PR pro.

Next, they'll help you find the newsworthy angle

As we discussed earlier, everyone has a story to tell, just as each company has a unique perspective and something of value to tell anyone listening. A solid PR strategy will identify several newsworthy angles for your business and then roll them out over time. I usually recommend ongoing pitching to the news media continually while issuing one news release via a wire service and a guest article as often as is feasible.

Unlike having a story placed in the news, a guest article, also often called a 'guest column', is content you create and then offer to appropriate news outlets. Many publishers producing magazines and newspapers, print, news websites with or without blogs, and podcast and streaming video producers are happy to get free high quality content and will tell you quickly if your story is of interest.

Then they'll create high-quality content for you

Although you might enjoy writing and be proficient at it, a full service public relations firm offers copywriting services. You should take advantage of having professional writers at your disposal. (They'll often gladly help you with your website content, brochures, social media posts, sales emails and other writing tasks you need handled). How content is written is just as important as what it contains. Top PR writers are often former journalists, which ensures your story is ready for use by a news outlet. To understand which writing conventions are expected in the news industry, read about the Associated Press Stylebook guidelines here. Virtually all legitimate news organizations (at least those producing print or electronic news) want pitches and articles compliant with these rules.

The other factor to have your PR agency prepare your content is the volume needed for a successful campaign. The likelihood is you're simply too busy to produce 10 to 12 news releases and articles annually, not to mention guest columns, interview scripts, and other materials essential to telling your story and creating an ongoing narrative in the news.

They'll identify interview subjects

The most effective public relations programs don't rely only on statements just from you and your spokesperson (if you have one). Well-written and compelling news releases include quotes from others, usually industry thought leaders, experts from trade associations and academia,

and anyone with relevance and credibility to support the main news theme of your content. Customer testimonials can be effective, too. However, because PR avoids self-promotional statements and tone, those advocating your value statements must be doing so in a manner suitable for a news report.

To gain coverage, they'll pitch the story

The best news story of the century is useless unless it gets reported. The pitching process and landing placement is where insisting on high quality content pays off. Even highly newsworthy and expertly prepared pitches are ignored or turned down by most editors and reporters. Your PR agency will already have contacts in the news business and a massive media database such as Cision. Also, the professionals on staff will be highly knowledgeable in how to craft email pitches and other tactics to ensure your story is noticed, and perhaps even read fully. They also will leverage resources such as HARO (Help A Reporter Out), Qwoted, and other channels used by reporters and freelance writers to find people to quote on various topics.

As is true in sales, pitching is a numbers game. Getting one recipient of your pitch in 10 to say "maybe" is an excellent batting average. It often takes hundreds of emails and Twitter messages and dozens of phone calls to garner just two or three uses of your story. However, if the one you impress and get a "yes" form is Forbes, Bloomberg, the Wall Street Journal, TechCrunch, a major news program, or the New York Times, that's all it takes to realize serious ROI for your PR budget.

Follow through on the pick up

Once an editor or reporter has indicated they want to run with your story, the job of the PR expert you're working with is not over. It's up to them to provide exactly what the newsperson wants to write and then publish the news item. Access to interview subjects, high resolution photos, videos, sometimes a product sample, or a telephone call or a screen sharing session to gather more information. Oftentimes the reporter is on a deadline, so promptly responding to their requests is crucial. Being forthright and candid in every way is key to earning the trust of those providing coverage and getting over the goal line. It's not unusual for a news outlet to do a follow-up story down the road, so exhibiting professionalism in every way pays big dividends now and in the future.

What's next? At this point you'll be enjoying seeing your name and company in the news and, hopefully, reviewing your Google metrics to measure the big jump in traffic to your website and the resulting impact in your sales figures. Keep in mind, however, that successful PR programs don't end with a few placements. To maximize the benefit of including public relations in your marketing efforts, you'll want to continue the process, month after month and indefinitely as long as you see the upside you expect.

5 Ways to Successfully Scale Your Business

An Interview with Jason Miller

Keep everything simple: Complication in any business development plan or strategy leads to overload and overload leads to failure. If a third grader can understand what you do and how you do it, then it's a win. I often see companies create complex applications that solve a lot of problems, but they can't explain how it works in an effective way. If the market doesn't understand it, they won't buy it.

The journey for the Strategic Advisor Board started five years ago. I had recently retired from the military and wanted to get into consulting businesses. Building strategic business models was a huge strength of mine as I had operated many companies while serving in the military.

Back then it was just me working with companies and helping them grow and scale. I knew that I would eventually need to surround myself with experts in many fields at some point. So, the birth of SAB or the Strategic Advisor Board happened. The team is amazing with the skillsets to help any company grow, scale, and win.

The journey of starting the Strategic Advisor Board was one of my most challenging projects to date. I had to find all the right people that had the knowledge and skillsets to become a part of such

a powerful machine. It took me over 8 months to find the talent that is currently on the Strategic Advisor Board team today. That careful selection process is what now sets us apart as a premier, results-based, rapid-revenue-creating team for any company wanting to grow and scale fast.

You've had a remarkable career journey. Can you highlight a key decision in your career that helped you get to where you are today?

One of the most key decisions I have had to make was actually pivoting out of being a Solo strategist into a model where I had equal shareholders that had their own superpowers to support the greater scale of the company. I had to literally interview hundreds of CEOs to find the right faces to put in the seats on the bus. The key "Choices" were critical as I had to align a successful balance between each 10 directors that would make the most sense for client success.

What's the most impactful initiative you've led that you're particularly proud of?

Without question, my most impactful initiatives have been our take a Veteran Off the Street Program and also our book launches that support heroes in need. Those are the things that are most impactful and they leave a massive footprint behind. I have always leveraged my companies to do a massive amount of good in the veteran community and will continue to do so.

Sometimes our mistakes can be our greatest teachers. Can you share a mistake you've made and the lesson you took away from it?

Business in general is never a smooth road. If it were, everyone would be doing it. We have gone through our moments like any other company. The Pandemic obviously had many impacts on every company in the marketplace. What I will say is this, having the power of "Team" is what helped us level up which in turn contributed to helping the companies we worked with level up as well.

Owning and running a company will always have its challenges. When people are involved, there is always room for failure. But failure is part of the learning experience and it only makes us better in the end. When you have a high-powered team like the Strategic Advisor Board there is only room for upward momentum. Being a CEO or business owner can be a very lonely place to be. I have found that being

the Founder/CEO of the Strategic Advisor Board is the exact opposite as we truly are the power of 10. One of the biggest mistakes I made in the past is choosing the wrong team. I put all the wrong people in the wrong seats and in the end I learned to slow down, take the time to put the work in and find the right people the first time.

How has mentorship played a role in your career, whether receiving mentorship or offering it to others?

Mentorship is key to success in life and business because they are very inter tangled. Your business plan should in turn support your total life plan. I have mentored thousands and thousands of minds over the course of 25 years.

It's critical both ways to mentor and be mentored as a lifelong learner yourself. If you want to become a 9-figure earner then you seek someone who has already accomplished that in their lifetime. I always say, seek knowledge through the power of mentorship and find the right person that makes sense for you.

Developing your leadership style takes time and practice. Who do you model your leadership style after? What are some key character traits you try to emulate?

Hands down my father and for many reasons. We didn't always agree on things but he has always been there to mentor and guide me. He was an entrepreneur himself his entire life and also a Vietnam veteran and my inspiration to serve to retire myself. He instilled honor, duty, respect, and selflessness into me as a young man and gave me an ethical playbook that I have lived with my entire life. I try not to emulate anyone, as my father always told me growing up, never emulate another, forge your own path and figure out who you are and what impact you want to make in this world.

Based on your experience, can you share with our readers the ways to successfully scale their business?

As the Founder and CEO of the Strategic Advisor Board, I am often asked this very question by new CEOs and established CEOs alike. Success can be measured in many ways, such as the efficacy of your overall strategy, strategic approaches, pivots, micro pivots, strategic implementation, or just time in business. It's a challenge to narrow success down into a few words, but one of my golden rules is to just keep it simple. This has always worked for me, so let's start with that.

1. **Keep everything simple:** Complication in any business development plan or strategy leads to overload and overload leads to failure. If a third grader can understand what you do and how you do it, then it's a win. I often see companies create complex applications that solve a lot of problems, but they can't explain how it works in an effective way. If the market doesn't understand it, they won't buy it!

2. **Stop talking about how great you are:** At the end of the day, the consumer doesn't care about your company. They have come to you for a service or product. Focus on the customer and explain the WIFM (what's in it for me) to them and credit your customers for your successes. Stop focusing on the ME, ME, ME strategy. Get engaged with crediting your customer for all your wins. It's intoxicating to see your customers support your brand, and it will drive you harder and faster.

3. **Surround yourself with the right people:** We all have our strengths and weaknesses. Know yours as the CEO and settle into your strategic

role. DO NOT take on things that don't fit into your superpower and delegate those down immediately. Focus on putting the right faces in the right seats on the bus to get things done. Staffing is super important and getting that right will support cross-functional team success in your company.

4. **Nail down your processes sooner than later:** Know your processes from acquisition all the way to asking for referrals and everything in between. An efficient and effective set of processes that support the entire customer journey is super important. If you are continuously "guessing" at this process, it will lead to bottlenecks and tons of lost revenue every single year. A/B split test multiple pipelines and work the bugs out of the one that works most effectively for your model.

5. **Document and leading from the front:** This is critical for the success of any company. Documentation of every staff position and title is extremely important. It's what allows you to hold all personnel accountable for the positions they hold. Counsel, guide, or mentor — you will miss the mark from time to time. Lead with integrity and always lead from the front. Document your own position as the CEO so your C-Suite knows what to expect from you daily and the superpowers you bring to the table.

There are many factors that lead to the success of a CEO. I have only lightly brushed on a few that have helped me stay focused and keep the company growing through each phase of the business life cycle. In my mind, one of the major areas that makes all the difference is having a team like the Strategic Advisor Board on your side guiding you through the rough waters will increase your success many times over.

It's important to guide your company along as the CEO. Look for the pathways to pivot where needed to support the next growth phase of your company and become the powerhouse that you first envisioned when you opened the doors.

Along with the five tips above, look at your process from end to end and see if you have a process for the following:

Acquisition: Do you have multiple processes to acquire new clients?

Sales: Do you have a successful sales process that feeds your machine?

Onboarding: Do you have a successful process for smooth onboarding of new customers?

Support: Do you have a customer support team that is on top of customer issues and concerns?

Communication: How do you effectively communicate with your customers when they need you?

Fulfillment: Are your fulfillment processes rock solid and can you deliver on time every time?

Referral Program: Do you have a way to reward people for being your biggest cheerleaders?

Most of all, are your own internal processes and procedures in place to support these simple steps? We often forget to do that bit of house cleaning every quarter to ensure we are still on track as we grow our business.

Operations shift and change; make sure you continue to put the right strategy in place to support growth (people and processes) and scale (monetary) sides of the business in sequence. Hold yourself accountable as the business owner and remember always, when you know better, you do better. Doing a ton of good in the world will always be the best practice for reaching success in your company.

What are some mistakes companies make when they try to scale a business?

There are way too many to name them in any order for sure. Two common ones are "growth vs scale. Many companies either overgrow in staff and under-scale in cash flow, which affects every area of the business. Or vice versa where it can have a drastic impact on the fulfillment process due to lack of proper staffing. The answer to fixing this is unfortunately very complicated but as a general rule of thumb try to keep your company balanced. If you balance the workload properly and keep your company as lean as possible in

every aspect it can reduce the chance of imbalance drastically.

Scaling includes bringing new people into the organization. How can a company preserve its company culture and ethos when new people are brought in?

In my mind it's very simple. We treat others as we want to be treated. Culture an environment of trust and harmony that is top driven from the C-suite all the way down to the lowest managers and staff. Your managers and senior leaders will take on your form of leadership in most cases so be careful not to enculture a leadership position that does not approach everything the same. Be firm, fair and consistent in all you do and live the values you preach to your staff and leadership.

A key aspect of scaling your business is scaling your team's knowledge and internal procedures. What tools or techniques have helped your teams be successfully scale internally?

There are a lot of them. This is an area that I could talk about all day. We continue to educate our workforce with training that matters and grows their ability to serve in higher positions of responsibility. Process development and documentation is the key element to being able to scale a company period. Taking those key elements and creating digital pipelines will not only reduce complication but give your staff the ability to grow the process for you. I also believe in keeping the processes extremely simple. This allows your process to grow and micro-pivot with your company and the staff very quickly. When all these parts come together it allows a smooth transition from one lifecycle to the next in business.

What do you recommend for onboarding new hires?

We have a very hands on approach to onboarding. We keep our process very personalized to make the new onboard feel like they are a part of the family right from the start. Everything is done with a hands on manual approach to maintain the personal contact and ability to stay connected through the process. This cultivates trust and respect immediately as they don't feel like another "Hire" that day. They feel like they are an instant part of the team.

Because of your role, you are a person of significant influence. If you could inspire a movement that would bring the most amount of good to the most people, what would that be?

I spend a lot of time with young people showing them that there is more to life than disconnected communication through devices. I feel the biggest aspect of improvement we can have as humanity is to just do a digital detox once a day. Stop what you are doing and just have a cup of copy with another human at a table without an electronic in your hand. The social impact on that small thing alone is far greater than one may think.

How can our readers further follow your work online?

- Website: strategicadvisorboard.com
- Instagram: instagram.com/strategicadvisorboard/
- Facebook: facebook.com/strategicadvisorboard
- Linkedin: www.linkedin.com/in/jasontmiller-sab
- YouTube: youtube.com/channel/UC6pqm8BJ1QsQWcMwjNJakEA
- Podcast: strategicadvisorboard.com/sab-podcasts

Jason Miller is the CEO of the Strategic Advisor Board which focuses on smart businesses growth in a changing environment. They focus on the customer and help their clients execute strategies as fast as possible. He is also the Founder and Chairman of Reliable Staff Solutions, a staffing agency that provides full-time and part-time staffing to companies that need remote work. Jason is also a three-time international bestselling published author with 7 published books. Jason donates all his book sales to "Homes for Heroes" of which donations have played a part in building multiple homes for wounded warriors.

Five Tips to Succeed as a Senior Executive

Shelby Jo Long

I have been in the world of communication for many years. I was a trained speaker in high school and college, I have been a professor and collegiate debate coach for 16 years, and I have been working with businesses on their internal culture and communication strategy for years. My background in public speaking and argumentation prepared me for work in brand strategy. Businesses need to differentiate their brand and create connections with clients in their internal and external messages.

I was ready to take my ideas out of the classroom and get into business operations. Communication is how we execute business operations and create relationships that sustain business. My business involvement now utilizes human communication as the catalyst for business growth. I am CEO of Business Dynamics with a focus on brand strategy and business culture, CEO of Rogue Publishing Partners that is an association of business partners to help people independently publish, and Senior VP of the Strategic Advisor Board, a business consulting group that develops revenue strategies for small business.

I have discovered the importance of your network in the business world. When starting a business, it is essential to use the network you already must build the foundation for your business. Building a new network is important for growing your business. You need new clients to grow your bottom line. Your business network then becomes key to taking your business beyond your own capabilities. Your network can help your business expand beyond where you thought possible.

There are so many opportunities when you build your network and expand your business relationships. Your network is truly your net worth.

One of the mistakes I made that was frustrating at the time but is funny in hindsight. I tried to be someone that I wasn't.

When I first started a business, I searched for the quick fix to get clients. Using methods that worked for other people helped me start my business, but it wasn't a way to build a solid foundation in my business. When I began to trust myself and my own expertise is when I developed my own methods to create a foundation for my business. I learned to trust myself and my intuition in business.

CEO responsibilities

The CEO serves the leader and manager role. Managers make sure that all business operations are efficient and productive. Leaders inspire and motivate people in the organization to work with optimum performance and creativity. That is, when CEOs begin to thrive, you feed the productivity and creative part of the organization.

"CEOs and executives are lonely" is a myth I hear frequently about the position. I believe it is lonely if you choose for it to be that way. CEOs that lead and inspire are involved with the business operations and connect with all parts of the business. That is easier as an executive for a small business, but I believe it to be true in larger organizations. The more involved a CEO is in all facets of the company creates an inspired business culture.

"CEOs know all the answers" is another myth I hear about the executive. A good CEO knows that they don't know all the answers and they will seek expert guidance and mentorship in the areas where they are not experts. Executive leaders answer for the organization, but don't need to be versed in all the areas to succeed.

Challenges faced by women executives

Many of the challenges for women in the executive come down to behavioral expectations which influence our behavior. As a society, we expect that male executives and female executives will communicate in certain ways because that is what we have witnessed. When 15% of Fortune 500 companies and about

20% of executives in other businesses are women, expectations are established by the frequency. There is a double bind for women in leadership. To be an effective leader, one needs to be direct, assertive, and confident. These qualities often create an unlikeable or harsh expectation of those women in executive positions. If a female executive tries to be more likable and personable in their approach, they are often perceived as 'soft' or not fulfilling the powerful position of the executive. The same expectations do not apply to male counterparts

Authority and credibility are extremely helpful in leadership positions, but relationship management is equally as important. You can be a great leader on paper but if you aren't displaying that in your interactions with other C-suite members or people in your organization, you won't be an effective leader. Leaders who focus on building relationships and providing value create an environment where CEO authority can be realized.

Certain traits are essential to be an effective leader, and not everyone possesses those traits. More importantly, not everyone wants to work on those traits. The most important trait is the desire to lead. The second is self-reflection. Each person has a certain charisma and speaker presence. A clear understanding of those strengths and weaknesses will set the foundation for you to grow and change with the requirements of the position. The final quality for leaders is to be ready to adapt and shift depending on your audience and function. Being nimble in your approach to leadership will allow you to make a bigger impact.

What I wish someone told me before I started

1. **Be ready for change every day.**
   Businesses must shift and adapt to meet the needs of clients, the marketplace and their own organization. A stoic business plan does not teach you how to shift to meet those needs.

2. **Your business is driven by customers.**
   You can have the best business plan or idea in the world, but if you can't bring in clients, you don't have a business.

3. **Trust in yourself.**
   Learning to trust your intuition in a professional business environment is challenging but will often lead you to the right answer. Follow your intuition, not the plans that have worked for others.

4. **Focus on your niche and offer first.**
   The more clarity you have in your offer, your audience and your own story in the beginning will save you time and money in marketing and increase your value in the marketplace.

5. **Building a business takes time.**
   The first business or idea that you launch needs to be situated in a market and adapted to a client base. This rarely happens on the first try, so be prepared for it to take time for your business to build.

I have been in college debate as a competitor and coach for many years. The activity has transformed the way I communicate and process information that explores multiple perspectives and solutions. The elements of competition, argumentation and having to respond in an efficient and concise manner have influenced how I function as a CEO and an executive. Most importantly, being in an environment where disagreement is commonplace, where comparisons between arguments and plans and weighing the impacts of decisions, have prepared me for the rigors of exploring decisions in the C-suite environment. It is important for us to be more comfortable with disagreement and discussion.

Better decisions will be made with this type of approach. Decisions will be made with active discussion, an exploration of the impacts and consequences of essential decisions. It is important for our youth and in decision making groups. That is the movement I would see making the biggest influence with current and future leaders.

Shelby Jo Long is an author, speaker, professor, and business strategist who helps businesses grow their brand. www.shelbyjolong.com

Telling Your Story is Only Half the Story

Joel Phillips

So, you landed that great interview with a major publication. Maybe you got on that podcast you have been trying so hard to become part of for the longest time. Perhaps you wrote an article and it got picked up so now you are published. Congratulations! Any one of these is a major accomplishment.

Even more inspirational is that person who wrote a book (or had one written for them) and has gotten it published, then sold to become a bestseller, or better yet, an international bestseller. You should absolutely be fighting for every piece of publicity you can get your hands on because that exposure creates two distinct realities.

First, every publication you become part of is an authority piece for you, your brand and your products or services. When you are published, it becomes recognized that you are an "expert" of sorts in whatever field you endeavor. An MD published in a medical journal, or a businessperson published in Pivot (or any other major publication) is given more credence and authority because their name is in print when compared to someone unpublished.

Think about it. On a level playing field, if you had to go to a doctor for a procedure, would you go to one who was published in a medical journal for that procedure, or would you choose the doctor who said they knew the procedure and had no validation to back up the claim? While there are many more factors at play, you would choose the published doctor on most days.

The second aspect of Public Relations is compounded authority. Each time you add authority by being published in an article, story, podcast or other media, you gain exposure. For every time you are featured speaking about a topic, you become better known for that topic and you reach the number of people equal to the number of people who read or listen to that publication. There may be minor spillover from those who encountered your media and shared it with their friends and colleagues, but as a rule, your audience is limited to circulation.

This is not a bad thing as the circulation for most major media is significant and can impact the product, service, organization, individual or idea you are promoting quite a bit, but you are still limited to that circulation. This exposure, even with inherited limitations, is still necessary for healthy business. Public Relations and media are even more vital today in a world full of noise where even well-known companies are struggling to be heard.

Syndication is the key

When you think of syndication, what comes to mind? More than likely, you think in terms of the magazine, podcast or publication being distributed over a wide network to many locations. This is great for overall exposure, but only for one instance when people read or listen to your publication before they move on to the next publication. The publishing organization, no matter who or how big it is, just does not have a mechanism to promote your article more than once before they move on.

Here is the kicker. That media you created is more than likely evergreen. What does that mean? It means that, even though it will only be promoted one time, it will exist in a dormant state until it is eventually rotated out, which could be months or even years that it will sit in mothballs doing you no good whatsoever.

There are two ways to keep this media alive. The first is to post it on every digital interaction you have. Why do you think people post "As Seen On..." all over the place? They do it because it keeps the publication alive and continues the cycle of authority building for any recipient encountering that media. You absolutely need to use your article everywhere you can and show the publisher logo like a badge of honor. After all, it is recognition of your expertise.

While this is a valid use of your media, there is still a substantial problem. This exposure is limited to your sphere of influence and most of the people in that sphere are already interacting with you and they know your expertise. You have already built trust with them. For those new to your sphere, these articles are validation and should boost your authority, trust and, therefore, sales.

Enter PASS. In our world, this acronym stands for Public Awareness Syndication Services and, while the phrase and its purpose may sound familiar, it is actually a newer construct built specifically for the purpose of promoting your publication across multiple channels and platforms. This promotion keeps your publication alive and delivering authority, even when nobody else is pushing your article any longer.

Imagine being able to extend the life of your authority piece and even exposing it to new audiences at the push of a button. Finally, you can take advantage of the evergreen nature of your publication while putting it in front of new faces every day. This is theoretically a simple concept, but very few people are putting that valuable piece of media to use beyond its original expiration date.

By extending the shelf life of your writing and increasing exposure metrics, you are taking your authority piece and transforming it into powerful advertising. You are using the value of the publication from a position of trust to generate more leads and potential sales than if you had just let the article sit or distributed it only to your sphere of influence.

It goes without saying that using PASS to take full advantage of your published media puts you light years ahead of your competitors and allows you to get the maximum mileage from your Public Relations efforts. This differentiation isn't a luxury in today's marketing environment. It is an absolute necessity.

If you have any questions or would like to learn more, visit us at www.proshark.com.

Audivita Studios Connects Your Voice to the World with its Powerful, Virtual Team Approach

David Wolf

Content reigns. And it's not so much the written word that people are devouring, but podcasts. About 30% of Americans listen to podcasts each week. It's revolutionizing how people spend their time.

It's not surprising that Amazon, Spotify and YouTube are making some strategic Podcast moves. Or that Conan O'Brien signed a $150 million podcast deal with SiriusXM. O'Brien's Team Coco has become a podcasting force, bringing in 180 million downloads a year.

David Wolf, founder of Audivita Studios, an audiobook, video and podcast production company in Albuquerque, New Mexico, is also navigating these new waters. "We're dancing with a dynamic, evolving, challenging market and it seems we're very much in step with it," he says. Come 2024, podcasts will make up 34.2% of US digital audio services ad spending at $2.56 billion.

"It all starts with audience development," says Wolf, whose previous company, Crywolf Productions, Inc. (1985–1999) and its recording studios provided music, sound design and production services for advertising and studios like Amblin, Discovery Channel, NBC Universal, and Disney, along other well-known brands.

Many startup podcasters are anxious to monetize their content with advertising.

"No advertiser is going to pay you for zero audience," says Wolf. "There are 5 million podcast series out there and 63 million separate episodes out there. But only half of them have been listened to 26 times. 2% are killing it, while the rest of the podcasts aren't. We are looking at how our podcasters can solve that problem."

The key is creating programs that meet the demand of the diverse podcast audience as podcasts help advertisers reach an even broader consumer audience. Podcast ad spending is slated to surpass $2 billion in 2023 and $5 billion by 2026.

Arguably, any entity can have a podcast. From DIY on Anchor to working with a company like Audivita that is full service, helping create the series. Today, Audivita has 50 podcast series in production on their network, spanning genres such as real estate, leadership, cloud computing, virtual CFO's, macular degeneration, mental health and more.

"Our current network of shows is designed to move the needle on whatever our client's backend business is and help them grow that business with the content they produce with us," says Wolf.

But what makes a podcast a hit is original content tapped into the cultural zeitgeist. And Wolf's "Audivita Originals" plans to do just that.

"In addition to producing podcasts that are designed to grow a business, Audivita Originals are entertainment podcasts, a very different animal, and an exciting place to be growing," says Wolf. "We are co-developing from the ground up, with a plan to build a sizable audience," he says. "Due to the caliber of talent and the popularity of the subject matter, it seems achievable." The Audivita Originals podcasts currently in production are "Evolutions Per Minute," an engaging deep dive into the influence of hip hop on jazz and vice versa and "Stories in the Room," conversations with the players who contributed to Michael Jackson's *Thriller* album.

"To promote the Originals podcasts we'll create a plethora of video clips that will be extracted from the episodes to promote each series on multiple social media channels, all moving toward creating partnerships and sponsorships to support production and drive revenue," says Wolf. "At a certain point, when you get between 6,000 to 10,000 streams per episode, then you can step into a zone where you can bring in some sponsorships and start charging for the exposure."

"We're a virtual company so our below the line expenses is purely soft," says Wolf. The Audivita team is composed of producers and audio editors with extensive experience producing audio for film, television and multimedia. Shaun Hettinger heads the podcast production team of Audivita. He brings years of experience composing music and creating audio for film, TV and multimedia, all of which informs how he designs the listener experience. When he's not producing podcasts for Audivita, he composes TV and film scores for clients like Amazon, YouTube, MTV, Gatorade, Revlon, Keeping Up with the Kardashians, The Hallmark Channel, and others. Shaun recently composed the theme song for Netflix's first ever nightly talk show: Chelsea Handler's "Chelsea."

"The production platforms we use are very light, which makes us nimble as a company and frees the cash up to explore and do other things," says Wolf.

Wolf also sees the growth potential in audiobooks. "Since 2015, the audiobook market has been growing at a rate of 25% to 28%," he says. "About 80,000 audio books were produced in 2021."

With one in eight books being an audiobook, Audivita produces hundreds of audiobook titles a year offering remote, virtual recordings of authors narrating their books (typically nonfiction) and also casting professional voice actors (typically fiction titles). Mark Shipman heads Audivita's Audiobook division. With forty years experience as a recording engineer and producer and more than three decades in marketing and business leadership, Mark has expertise to add to the production process. Whether you need a performance coach for author narration, or a professional narrator, Audivita offers it all.

Many authors are asking why they should consider producing an audiobook version of their title. "We tell our authors and publishers that we're unlocking a new audience that doesn't feel they have the time to sit and read. Whether it's time scarcity, energy scarcity or they just don't process information that way. These are people who would rather be listening while walking the dog or doing errands."

Much of Audivita's audiobook production business comes from partnering with publishers or publishing service providers that either recommend them or use their services as part of the publishers' brand. In this case, the publisher will hand their author off to Audivita for the recording, editing, casting, or recording of the author if they're reading the book themselves.

Business in the age of COVID has never been so fluid and flexible nor so far ranging when it comes to strategies to meet the content consumer on the go. No one is static. And Audivita is right in sync.

How Important Is Public Relations in My Business?

Do you know how important public relations in your business is? Public relations is extremely important for businesses of all sizes. It can help you build a positive reputation, reach new customers, and boost your bottom line.

In today's world, it's crucial for businesses to stay on top of their PR game. As a matter of fact, the best way to make sure that you're getting the most bang for your buck is by utilizing a public relations agency. PR experts will ensure that your company's brand is represented in the best possible light.

They also help you to find new ways to interact with your customers and potential customers. And will provide you with the tools and resources needed to communicate with the media and other influential people in your industry. Keep reading to uncover all aspects of public relations to grow your business.

How important is PR in your business?

Public Relations (PR) is important for the success of your business. It's the way you communicate with your audience. The first impression matters, and your company's public relations strategy is one of the key ways to make that first impression a good one.

Good public relations can improve your business's reputation, boost your sales, and even attract new customers. So, if you're not actively managing your company's PR, it's time to get started. Public relations aren't just for big companies and corporations.

It's for anyone who has a business to grow and wants to become more visible needs to consider public relations. Here are just a few reasons why public relations should be a key part of your business strategy:

- **Help you build a positive reputation.**

A strong public relations strategy can help you build a positive reputation for your business. It is important because your reputation can have a major impact on your bottom line. If customers and clients perceive your business in a positive light, they're more likely to do business with you. On the other hand, if your reputation is negative, it could dissuade potential customers from doing business with you.

- **Assist you in reaching new customers**

An effective public relations strategy can help you reach new customers and expand your customer base. It is because PR can help you generate positive media coverage for your business. And when people see your business in the news or in other positive light, they're more likely to consider doing business with you.

- **Boost your bottom line**

Because public relations can help you build a positive reputation and reach new customers, it can ultimately lead to increased sales and revenue for your business. If you're looking for a way to give your business a boost, public relations is a great place to start.

- **Become the customer's first preference**

When customers hear about you or your company, they often decide whether to buy from you based on the first impression they get. In fact, when people meet a company's public relations representative for the first time, they're almost three times more likely to choose that company over its competitors.

That means that the right public relations strategy can make or break your business, so you should start right away if you're not currently using public relations to build your reputation.

- **Improve your sales**

Your company's image and your customer service levels are both important factors that can influence customers' decisions about whether or not to buy from you. But if you want to really boost your sales, you need to consider how to communicate your company's strengths.

Companies with excellent customer service were more likely to get more sales. People like to buy from a company with a positive brand name, even if it costs more. If you want to attract more customers and increase your sales, then improving your company's public relations is a must.

- **Social media engagement**

When you use public relations for your business, you don't have to spend a ton of money. You can use free tools, such as Facebook and Twitter to help you spread the word about your brand.

You can also try paid marketing strategies like social ads, which are advertisements on social media that people can click on. You can also buy ads on Google or Instagram. You can also use email marketing to help you get in touch with potential customers.

- **Build business reach**

One of the most effective ways to increase your business's visibility is to attract new customers through your public relations efforts. When you advertise your company's products or services in the media, you get far more interest in those products than when you don't advertise at all.

The reason for this is simple: when you advertise, your company's name and services come to mind for your potential customers. And when they think about buying from you, they're more likely to do so if your company offers better products or services than its competitors.

When you advertise, you're telling potential customers that you offer something they want, and that makes them more likely to buy from you.

- **Increase business visibility**

The internet is an amazing tool for marketing your business, but you can only reach so many people using only one method. If your social media channels are the only place people can see your company, then you're missing out on a lot of potential customers.

So, when you use a variety of marketing methods, you're increasing your brand

awareness. People will see that you're different and unique, and you're giving them something different from what they would find elsewhere.

- **Build a loyal customer base**

The best way to attract new customers is to build loyalty among current customers. Loyalty is important because your current customers are more likely to tell their friends about you and recommend you to their family and friends.

They'll also buy from you more frequently, and more people will be exposed to your company's offers.

So, by building a strong public relations strategy, you can help your business to attract new customers and build loyalty among existing customers.

- **Improve your business branding**

People may not always know what your brand stands for, but if you don't promote yourself positively on social media, your audience won't know what you stand for. If you create content that's relevant to your audience, they'll know who you are.

They'll know what you're offering, and they'll want to hear what you have to say. So, by doing these things, you're establishing a strong connection with your audience.

As you can see, public relations is a vital part of any business strategy. If you're not utilizing PR to its full potential, you're missing out on a major opportunity to improve your business. So, if you want to take your business to the next level, make sure you put public relations at the top of your list.

How to build public relations

Building public relations means having a positive and negative impact on the public's minds. So, you need to know what your company stands for, who you should target, what kind of marketing strategies to adopt and so on.

First, you need to understand your company's purpose; you should know what the mission statement is and what your values and ethics are. After that, you should know who your company's customer is, what his needs are, and what kind of products he likes.

Then you should know what kind of products you're offering, what the benefits of your product are and so on. When you know the customer's needs, you can decide what kind of business strategy to adopt. It is the basis of building good public relations.

So, it's better to be prepared with all this information before starting to work on a project. Otherwise, it would be hard to make something out of nothing. Here's a step-by-step guide to building public relations for your business.

- Step 1: Start with your personal brand: Before you start any PR campaign, make sure that you have a clear understanding of who you are and what your brand is. It is also the first step to building a solid reputation for your business.

- Step 2: Choose your audience: Once you understand your brand, decide who you want to reach. Are you targeting a specific demographic? Do you want to target a certain type of person?
- Step 3: Determine your goals: Write down your goals. What do you want to accomplish with this campaign? What are you trying to achieve?
- Step 4: Develop a strategy: Now that you know your goals, determine your best strategy. What will be your best approach? What is your best way to reach your audience?
- Step 5: Develop a plan: Write down your plan. What are your strategies? How will you accomplish your goals? What are your tactics?
- Step 6: Create content: Now, it's to work on content creation. What is the purpose of your content? What is your message? Who is your audience?
- Step 7: Launch your campaign: Finally, you can launch your campaign. How will you reach your audience?

Can social media help your PR?

If you're thinking about improving your public relations, you should know that there are many ways to do so. You can create an online presence and make sure that your company's social media pages are set up properly.

Social media is a great way for you to get your message out. You can use it to connect with your customers and engage with them. You can also use it to share your business news and updates.

You might think that social media is a good way to market your business. However, it's not just a good way to market your business. It's a great way to build relationships with your customers. You can use it to talk to your customers and get feedback.

The last thing you can do is use social media to build relationships with your customers. You can create a Facebook group for your clients and give them the chance to ask questions.

How to use social media to improve PR

Social media has changed everything in the way we do business. Now, it is not only about posting content to your website but also about building relationships with your customers, potential clients, vendors, and partners.

To achieve these goals, you must use the right tools and techniques to connect with your audiences. Let us check out how you can use social media marketing tactics to increase your online presence.

1. Grow your business

Social media marketing is an effective way to grow your business. It helps you in connecting with your target audience through different social channels like Facebook, Instagram, Twitter, etc. It gives you the opportunity to create awareness about your products and services and engage with your audiences. It will eventually lead to increased sales.

2. Gain followers

Social media marketing is the best way to gain followers on various social platforms like Facebook, Instagram, Twitter, etc. Most businesses rely on these platforms to boost their visibility. It helps in creating a positive image about your brand and engaging with your followers.

3. Create awareness

Social media marketing provides you with an opportunity to create awareness about your brand. The more people know about you, the more people will follow you on social media.

4. Promote your products

Using social media to promote your products is a great way to connect with your audiences. Your followers and fans will help you spread the word about your product by sharing them on their social media accounts. It will increase the exposure of your brand and ultimately increase your sales.

5. Sell your services

Social media marketing is an effective way to sell your services to your target audiences. Through social media marketing, you can create awareness about your services, and you can also share the details of your services. It will lead to an increased conversion rate and ultimately help you in increasing your sales.

6. Enhance customer experience

Social media marketing provides you with an opportunity to interact with your customers. By using social media, you can get feedback about your products and services, and you can even solve the customer's problems.

All these things increase the customer experience and will eventually result in increased conversions. So, these were the 6 tactics to improve your public social relations.

Public relations is extremely important for businesses of all sizes. It can help you build a positive reputation, reach new customers, and boost your bottom line. In conclusion, PR is an important part of any business. A good PR will help you to make more money.

Best Practices for Getting Featured in Major Publications

Do you know the best practices for getting featured in major publications? Getting featured in major publications is a great way to build credibility and brand awareness and increase traffic to your website. There are many ways to increase your chances of being featured in a major publication.

- First, try to get involved with as many relevant online and offline communities as possible. It will help you build up a network of contacts who may be able to help promote your work.

- Additionally, be active on social media platforms and make sure to share your work regularly.
- Finally, always be professional and polite when interacting with potential customers or clients.

However, there are a lot of factors that come into play when deciding who will feature your company or product in their publication. So, let's learn some of the best practices for getting featured in major publications.

What are the best practices for getting featured in major publications?

The term "featured" refers to being in one of the top stories on a website. It means that someone is reading your story, and the publication is displaying it prominently. To achieve this, you need to get your story featured in the right publications.

There is no one-size-fits-all answer to this question, as the best way to get featured in a major publication will vary depending on your specific goals and objectives. However, there are some general best practices that can help increase your chances of being featured in a top-tier publication like:

1. Creating quality content that is interesting and informative
2. Reaching out to influential people in your industry or field
3. Building strong relationships with members of the media
4. Participating in relevant conferences or events
5. Getting involved with popular social media platforms

Getting featured is one of the most important ways to increase traffic to your site. When you get featured, you will usually have the option to share the link to your story, which means that more people will read your content. Here are the best practices that are really very effective for getting featured in major publications.

1. Create great content

If you are new to writing, it is important that you start off with a good story. People don't read or write stories just because they're bored. They read stories because they want to learn something or they want to find out about an interesting topic.

It's always better to create a story that you find interesting rather than trying to force yourself to write a story that you think people will want to read.

2. Choose the right publication

Next, you need to choose the right publication. A lot of people think that because they write a great piece of content, it is automatically published. Unfortunately, that is not true.

You need to make sure that you are choosing the right publication. You need to find out if there is a specific editor for your kind of content.

Sometimes, editors will only accept certain kinds of content. You can also check out who the editors are. Are they reputable? Are they well known for their quality?

When choosing the right publication, you need to focus on finding out how often the publication publishes. It will give you a rough idea of whether it is worth your time or not.

3. Be professional

Your story should be well written and should be free of grammatical errors. You can hire a professional writer who can make sure of the work quality and can perform the job for you.

4. Be confident and honest

Finally, you need to be honest and confident. You need to tell the editors that you are new to the business and are trying to get featured.

Tell the editors that there are many opportunities out there for people. If you approach them with confidence, you will stand out. Ask the editor for an interview and also send them a link to your article. It will show that you are interested in getting featured.

5. Make sure your content is unique

Another important thing to keep in mind is that you shouldn't copy. If you are using the same article that someone else has written on his website, then it will harm your reputation. It might also result in legal issues. You should also avoid plagiarism. So, make sure your content is unique and original.

How to identify the best publications in which to get featured

You need to do some research and find the best publications for getting featured. First, you need to know what kind of publications are available in the market. There are several types of publications, each having a different scope and niche.

Before you start searching for the publication you are interested in, you need to decide what you are looking for. Let's talk about some of the most common types of publications you can choose from.

1. Blogs

A blog is a great place to publish your content. They are one of the most popular publications today. And it is also very easy to submit your articles. Some people refer to blogs as micro-blogs. It means that the posts are very short and usually consist of links to other sources.

Blogs are the ideal platform for you to find new customers. They are designed to help people find content. And if you can write content that is helpful to them, they are sure to read it. And after reading, they are also likely to share it on their social media profiles.

There are many reasons why bloggers prefer blogging. The first reason is that it is very easy to get started. As long as you have the right software, you are ready to start creating your own blog. Once you get started, you can use the same blog template for years to come. And you can also publish content automatically. There are no technical issues involved.

However, there is also a downside. Most people who want to make money online prefer to publish their own content. And blogs are known to pay poorly. In fact, most bloggers are not making much money. But they do have a lot of followers and connections. So, if you can get them to connect with you, then you may be able to gain a lot of followers.

You can also make money by selling products to your readers. However, you will need to find a marketplace that allows you to sell to your readers. For instance, you can find many companies that will allow you to sell your products on their sites. You can also sell your products directly to your readers.

2. Online magazines

These are also referred to as ezines. They are more like print magazines than blogs. And they can often pay more for your content. These are good choices if you want to make a living out of writing. You can expect to make at least $25 for every 1,000 words you publish.

It is much higher than you can expect from blogs. And you can easily earn $100–$300 per article. However, it is important to note that these publications pay more when they have very good content.

Another reason why people like online magazines is because they are more professional. And most of them look much better than blogs. It means that your content is more likely to be read.

You can find online magazines by visiting online communities. You can also search for specific keywords on Google or Yahoo.

3. Social media platforms

Social media platforms are great places to share your content. And you can make a lot of money if you are good at writing. Many people are making a full-time living from writing on these sites. You can also make some money by promoting other people's content. It is how the affiliate marketing model works.

4. Ebooks

Ebooks are also a very popular type of publication. You can find thousands of ebook publishers in the online market. And each one has its own rules and regulations. However, most publishers require you to put a certain number of words in your book.

Ebooks are great for promoting your product and for marketing. You can use them to sell your product. And you can also use them to promote your website. You can also use them to connect with your audience.

5. Podcasts

Podcasts are audio and video recordings. You can find them on the web, on YouTube, and on iTunes. And these days, they are becoming increasingly popular. You can use podcasts to promote your own products.

You can also use them to give your readers advice. In summary, there are many different types of publications you can choose from. Some of them are more popular than others. And some are better suited for your niche.

Benefits of getting featured in major publications

As a business owner, you are always looking for ways to get your company noticed. One way to do this is to get featured in major publications. It can help you reach a wider audience and generate more leads.

It's no secret that being featured in a major publication can do wonders for your career and your business. But what about the personal benefits of having a big name on your resume? The truth is that it is the best way to get noticed in your industry and start building a solid reputation.

A lot of people have asked me whether it's worth the effort to get featured in a major publication. If you're wondering whether it's worthwhile to get featured in a major publication. Here are some of the benefits of getting featured in major publications:

1. **Increased exposure and boost in authority**

One of the main benefits of getting featured in a major publication is that it will give you increased exposure. It can help you attract new customers and clients who may not have heard of your business before.

Getting featured in a reputable publication can also help boost your authority and credibility. It can make it easier to close sales and win over new clients.

2. **Greater reach and improved SEO**

Another benefit of being featured in a major publication is that it gives you a greater reach. You will be able to reach more people and potentially generate more leads.

Getting featured in a major publication can also help improve your SEO. It can lead to more traffic and higher rankings in search engines.

3. **Enhanced branding and brand awareness**

Finally, getting featured in a major publication can help enhance your branding. It can make it easier for people to remember your company and what it stands for.

When your company gets featured in a major publication, it gets hundreds of thousands of impressions in a single day. It means that your company's profile gets out there in the most effective way possible.

You'll notice that your name will be listed on the publication's website, along with your company's. When people visit the blog, they'll read about you and your company.

4. **Help build trust and credibility**

When people see your name in a major publication, they'll know that you are a well-known expert in your field. It makes you look like a legitimate source of information. Even if you don't sell anything, you'll still gain credibility. People will assume that you are a trustworthy source of information and products.

5. **Brand growth**

One of the best ways to build a brand is to be featured in a major publication. When people search for your company's name, they'll be directed to your company's website.

You'll notice that your company's brand will start to grow. People will start to associate your company's name with quality and credibility.

6. More leads

As you are featured in a major publication, you'll be seen by thousands of new people. Being featured in a major publication can help you get more leads and sales.

7. More exposure to social media

Getting featured in a major publication can help you gain more exposure on social media sites. When you're featured in a major publication, you'll be mentioned in articles and news stories. It can drive traffic to your social media sites. It means that you'll get more followers and engagement on your social media sites.

Conclusion

In conclusion, the best way to get featured in a major publication is to build your brand and reputation first. Then, once you have that, you can focus on the other aspects of the publication's editorial calendar.

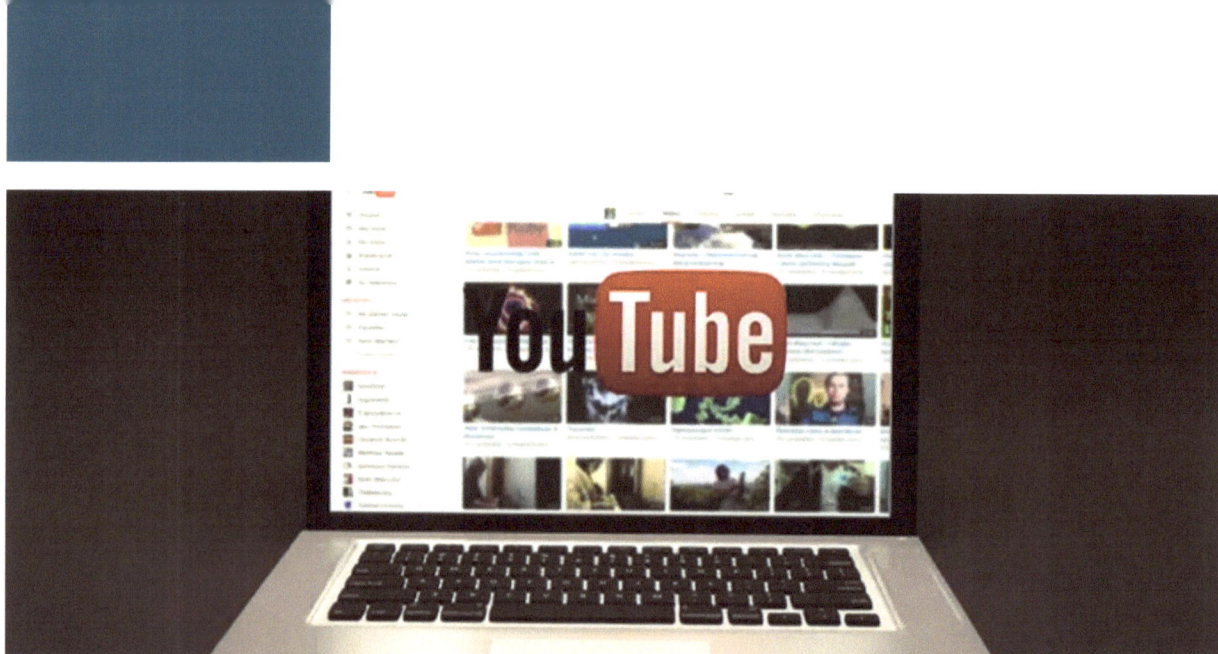

How to Create a YouTube Channel for Business

The world of social media is evolving, and so is the way we market our businesses. YouTube is one of the best platforms for businesses looking to reach an audience and connect with customers. Creating a YouTube channel for your business can help you build credibility and visibility, and it can be a great way to promote your products and services.

YouTube has now become the second-largest search engine after Google. Millions of people use YouTube to search for information and entertainment. More than 5 billion hours of video are watched every month.

What is a YouTube channel?

A YouTube channel is a collection of videos uploaded by a single person or organization. The individual or group creates them, and they are shared on YouTube.

A channel can be anything from music to comedy to cooking to news to gaming. There are over a billion channels on YouTube, so there is something for everyone.

The best part about a YouTube channel is that it's free. You don't have to pay for the video content. The videos are all free, and the only thing you have to do is create them.

Create a YouTube channel for business

There are many YouTube channels available that are used by businesses to showcase their products and services. Many companies start their own channel to promote their business. For example, plenty of online stores such as Amazon and eBay run their own YouTube channel to share tips on selling products and promoting their brand.

Here are some ways that you can create a YouTube channel for business.

1. Start with the right content

The first thing that you need to do is pick a topic that you will cover. You should decide on what kind of topics you would like to talk about. You can also choose a topic that you know a lot about and discuss it. It would help if you chose topics that will keep people engaged.

Some of the things that you should consider are:

- The type of videos that you want to make
- What types of videos are popular?
- What type of people visits your website?
- Do you offer any special deals or incentives for subscribing to your channel?
- What are the keywords that people are searching for?

Once you have determined what your channel will cover, you can start creating content. Content creation is one of the most challenging aspects of starting a YouTube channel. Some people think that they can create great content within minutes. Unfortunately, this isn't the case. Creating great content takes time and effort.

You need to make sure that you write content that will interest your audience.

You can use tools such as Keywords Everywhere to find out what people are searching for.

2. Create the perfect title

Creating the perfect title is crucial. People spend only a few seconds scanning through YouTube videos. Therefore, viewers will quickly skip over the video if the title is not compelling. It would be best if you made sure that the title is catchy and exciting. You can use tools such as HootSuite to help you come up with ideas for the title.

You need to remember that the title needs to be brief and straightforward. Ensure that you include the keywords you have selected for your channel. Also, make sure that the title includes the name of your business. Your channel name will be included at the beginning of the title. It is where you want to put your business name.

3. Create a beautiful profile picture

A beautiful profile picture is essential. You need to use a profile picture that represents your brand. Most people scan YouTube videos quickly. Therefore, you need to make sure that your profile picture stands out. You can use tools such as PicMonkey to create a beautiful profile picture.

You can also upload a picture that you have taken yourself. Make sure that you use a profile picture that is relevant to your business.

4. Create a professionally designed cover

People are bombarded with information every day. Therefore, your YouTube channel must look attractive and professional. The best way to achieve this is to hire a professional designer. They can help you come up with a unique design that will make your channel stand out from the rest.

5. Create a logo

Your logo is the face of your YouTube channel. You must create a logo that represents your brand. You can use tools such as Canva to create a logo. You can also use a graphic design program such as Photoshop to create a logo.

6. Choose the right tags

Tags are the words that appear next to the videos. The more people click on your tag, the higher your rank. You need to create a list of tags that people will click on. These include the name of your business, your category, and the type of videos that you are making. You can use tools such as Google Adwords to determine the popularity of different tags.

7. Add a description

The description appears on the side of the videos. You need to make sure that it is short and easy to read. You should also add the keywords that you want to rank for. You can use tools such as HootSuite to add a description.

8. Create the perfect thumbnail

Thumbnails are the images that appear on the right side of the videos. Thumbnail images should be high quality and look professional.

9. Create a custom channel page

People are bombarded with information every day. Therefore, they want to quickly find the videos that they are interested in watching. If you don't have a custom channel page, people will not be able to find your channel. You can use tools such as WordPress to create a custom channel page.

10. Add videos to your playlist

You can also add your videos to playlists. Playlists allow people to watch related videos. You can create playlists for different categories such as:

- Videos for beginners
- Videos about your business
- How-to videos

How to use social media to promote your YouTube channel

1. A YouTube channel is an excellent way to promote your business. It's a free platform that allows you to create videos and share them. You can also use it to share your content and products.
2. Make sure you have a strong niche: If you're using YouTube to promote your business, you'll want to make sure you have a strong niche. You can also use Google Trends to find out what your audience is interested in and then create a video.
3. Create engaging videos: You don't need to spend a fortune on video production to create an effective YouTube channel. The key is to create videos that are interesting and engaging. You can do this by

interviewing people who work in your industry or creating videos showing how your products can be used.

4. Use video marketing tools: Once you've created your videos, you'll want to make sure you use the right tools to promote them. You can use the YouTube analytics tool to see which videos are performing well, and you can use the Google Adwords tool for advertising your videos on social media.

5. Promote your videos: Once you've created them, it's time to promote them. You'll need to use social media to share them, and you can also create an email list to send your videos to.

6. Grow your audience: You can also use YouTube to grow your audience. You can create a playlist of your best videos, and you can use the YouTube search tool to find out which videos have performed well in the past. You can then add these videos to your channel and you can share them on social media.

7. Keep your channel updated: You'll want to make sure you keep your channel updated and that you regularly share new videos. You can do this by sharing new videos or by creating new videos.

8. Get creative: You don't need to stick to business-related topics when you're using YouTube. You can use the platform to promote your hobbies or to share content about your favourite topics.

9. Create a schedule: If you want to use YouTube to promote your business, you'll need to create a schedule for your videos. You can create a weekly schedule or a monthly schedule.

10. Use it to promote your products: YouTube can also promote your products. You can create a playlist of your best videos, and you can use the YouTube search tool to find out which videos have performed well in the past. You can then add these videos to your channel and you can share them on social media.

Tips to consider while making a YouTube channel

- Make sure you have a good microphone, camera, and editing software
- Have a good and interesting topic to talk about
- Use your creativity to make it unique
- Create content that is informative and entertaining
- Share your videos with friends and family
- Start making videos and let your creativity flow
- Try to make it as entertaining as possible
- Don't forget to tag your videos with the proper keywords
- Always put a link to your channel in the description of your video
- Comment on other people's videos and help them out

YouTube Shorts and how to use them

YouTube Shorts are a series of videos that are uploaded to YouTube. They are short and have a limited run. They are created to be used in a variety of ways. They can be used as a standalone piece of content, or they can be used as part of a campaign.

A Short is short

A short usually lasts between three to ten minutes. They are created to be used in a variety of ways. A short can be used as a standalone piece of content, or it can be used as part of a campaign.

YouTube Shorts are a type of branded content that YouTube introduced. It is a new way to engage with your audience. It is a good option for brands who want to connect with their audience through video.

How to use YouTube Shorts

YouTube Shorts are a great way to tell stories. They are a great way to share stories. They can be used for a variety of purposes. You can use them to promote your business; they could be used to teach people something; they can be used to entertain people; they can be used to inform people.

They can be used in many ways and for a variety of purposes. They can be used as standalone content, or they can be used as part of a campaign.

How to build a following on YouTube

You can build a following by posting videos, uploading pictures, or making other types of content. The key is to keep creating and sharing content.

Your videos should be high quality, engaging, and well-edited. You can use any camera you have. Just make sure that your content is high-quality.

You should include some kind of introduction to your video. This will help people know what they're about to see.

You can also add subtitles if you need to. This will help people who are watching your videos in other languages.

Wrapping it all up

Now you can easily create your own YouTube channel. The most important thing about your video is that it has to be entertaining. People will not watch a video that they don't like. If you want to create a channel for your business, you need to ensure that the videos you upload are fun, engaging, and entertaining. If you don't have a strong personality, then you won't be able to create a channel that people will like.

Remember that it takes time and effort to create a great channel. Therefore, it is crucial that you invest time and effort. It is a great way to promote your business.

Is Using Social Media Still an Effective Tool for Business?

Social media is everywhere, and it's almost always being used in some way or another to promote a business.

Social media is one of the most effective marketing tools available today, but how do you get started? If you're just getting started or already using social media, this post will help you determine whether it's still a good fit for your business.

What exactly is social media?

Social media is a term that describes a group of online services that are designed to connect people through the exchange of ideas, information, and content. The primary purpose of social media is to connect people. There are many different types of social media. Some of the most popular include Facebook, Twitter, YouTube, Instagram, Pinterest, LinkedIn, Reddit, TikTok, and Snapchat.

Social media is essential because it allows you to stay in touch with people in your life. You can post pictures, videos, and updates about yourself, your friends, and your family. Social media is a great way to keep up with friends, family, and business contacts.

Is social media still effective?

Social media marketing has been around for a while now, and businesses are still using it to generate leads, drive traffic to their site, and increase sales. However, many people are becoming wary of using social media and feel that they do not get any return on their investment. Is there a reason for this?

If you want to generate leads, drive traffic to your website or increase sales, you should use social media. However, if you feel that social media is too expensive, you may be right. For most businesses, social media is very cost-effective. You can quickly get started for free. If you are new to social media, you can even start with free Facebook.

So what are the main benefits of using social media for your business?

1. Get started for free

The first benefit of social media is that it is free to use. You don't need to spend a penny to get started. There is no minimum number of followers required to sign up. All you need is to create an account. Then, you can start posting. You can choose to post about your product or service, promote your website, share links to articles you found exciting, and much more.

You can easily find new customers on social media because you will be able to reach them via different channels. You can even use social media to sell to them. Most social media platforms allow you to share links to products or services. You can offer a discount on those products or services and let potential customers know about them.

For instance, you can share an article about a new book you read and let your followers know about it. Or, you can share an article

about a new restaurant you found and recommend that people try it out.

When you share a link to a product or service on social media, you essentially give it away for free. It will give you exposure. As long as you are willing to put in the effort, you can achieve great results with minimal effort.

2. Build relationships

Social media can help you build relationships. When you connect with other people, you will be able to exchange ideas and opinions. You can find valuable contacts that can help you get work done. It can also help you gain referrals. You can ask your friends, family members, and colleagues to like your page and share it on their timelines.

You can also use social media to promote your business. You can post updates about upcoming events, contests, discounts, or new services on your page. You can also share your company's news and announcements on your page.

You can also find customers on social media. You can start conversations with potential customers and convert them into customers. They may already be interested in your product or service. You need to reach out to them.

3. Create brand awareness

Another benefit of social media is that it can help you build brand awareness. When you are on social media, you share your company information, which is a great way to build brand awareness.

You can share links to your website, blog posts, photos, and videos. When people share your posts on their timelines, they can tell their friends and family about you. You can also use social media to promote your products or services. You can share links to them on your page and ask your followers to share them on their timelines.

4. Drive traffic to your website

One of the most significant benefits of social media is that it can help you drive traffic to your website. People share articles and other content on social media. When people share these things, they can direct their friends to your website. You can then have them visit your site and see what you offer.

When you drive traffic to your website, you are getting backlinks. Backlinks are essential because they help search engines rank your website. Your website's ranking will improve.

5. Generate leads

A huge benefit of social media is that it can help you generate leads. People on social media are more likely to buy from companies that they follow. If you post about new products, they will see your message and might be interested in buying from you.

6. Increase sales

You can also use social media to increase sales. You can use it to share coupons, offers, and other deals. You can also share your company's news and announcements on your page. People can then see your offers and buy your products.

How to use social media for your business

You might be thinking, 'Why do I need to use social media for my business?' Well, as we know, Social media is an excellent way of connecting with your target audience. It's also a great way to create a buzz around your brand. It is an excellent way to get your name out there and make sure people know your brand.

1. Create a strategy: Before you start using social media for your business, you'll want to create a strategy. It will help you decide what you want to use social media for and how you want to use it. You might want to create a blog or a Facebook page, or you might want to use Twitter.
2. Start using it: Once you've decided on a plan, you'll want to start using social media. You can use tools like Hootsuite or Buffer to manage your social media accounts. You can also use social media platforms like LinkedIn and Facebook to reach your target audience.
3. Keep it up: If you want your social media efforts to be practical, you'll need to keep using it. That means you'll need to make sure you're posting regularly and creating engaging content.
4. Get feedback: If you want to know if your social media efforts are working, you can ask your customers or clients for feedback.

You can also ask them if they'd recommend your business.

5. Don't forget about SEO: You should always consider your search engine optimization (SEO) strategy. You can read more about this in the SEO section of our blog.

The best social media marketing platforms

Social media marketing is an integral part of any successful business. It's how people find out about your business, learn about your products and services, and keep up with you and your brand. It's also a powerful tool to help increase sales.

The first step in using social media marketing is choosing the right platform for your business. It would help if you decided what platforms are most relevant for your business.

Facebook is by far the most popular social media site. It has over 1 billion monthly users and is the second most visited website in the world. It's also the largest social network by a number of users. Facebook is free to use, but there are a few costs associated with advertising on Facebook.

Twitter is a micro-blogging site that allows you to share short messages or "tweets" with your followers. Twitter is one of the most popular social networks for businesses, especially those in the technology and entertainment industries. Twitter can be used to post news stories, announcements, and updates about your business.

LinkedIn is a professional networking site where users can connect and exchange information with other professionals. LinkedIn is an excellent platform for companies looking to connect with other businesses and individuals. The site also has a lot of valuable features to help users grow their professional network.

YouTube is a video-sharing website owned by Google. It's one of the most popular websites on the internet. YouTube is an excellent platform for businesses that want to upload videos and share them with their followers. You can even make money by selling advertising space on your videos.

Instagram is an app that allows you to take photos and add text, hashtags, and location information to them. Instagram is a great place for people who want to share photos of themselves and their surroundings. Many people use Instagram as a way to share lifestyle photos and posts about their daily lives. Instagram is free to use, but it does have some limitations. If you want to use Instagram as a tool for business, you'll need to pay for advertising space.

Snapchat is a mobile app that allows users to send pictures and videos that disappear after they're viewed. Snapchat is a great way to share photos and videos with your friends and followers. It's also a great platform for businesses to promote their products and services. Snapchat is free to use, but you can't make money from your content.

Top tips for using social media for business

The first thing you should do when starting a business is research your target market. You'll want to find out who your target market is and how they use social media.

1. Start with Facebook: You'll want to start with Facebook because it's the most popular social network. It's also a great place to start. If you want to be more successful, you'll need to start by getting your name out there.
2. Create a profile: Once you've decided on your target market, it's time to create a Facebook page. You'll want to make sure you have a professional-looking page.
3. Start posting: Now that you've created your Facebook page, it's time to start posting. Posting is one of the most effective ways to get your name out there. Make sure you have a clear message and post the correct type of content when you post.
4. Promote your business: Once you've started posting, it's time to promote your business. You can use paid advertising or promote your business through social media. Either way, you'll want to make sure you're reaching the right people.
5. Track your results: Once you've promoted your business, it's time to track your results. You'll want to see if you're getting any results. If not, you'll need to make changes to your strategy. You'll want to keep track of them if you are getting results.

In conclusion, there are several benefits to social media for businesses, including increased brand awareness, more leads, and better customer service. Social media has evolved from a tool to a toolset that allows businesses to interact with their customers in a new way. The ability to reach customers via social media is now part of the marketing mix, and it's become a necessary part of most marketing strategies. However, the most significant benefit of social media for business is the ability to interact with your customers. It's a great way to stay in touch with your customers and build relationships.

How Can I Benefit from PR in My Company

Public relations can help you build more relationships with your customers, increase the trust between your company and other corporations, and grow awareness for your company through different methods. In addition to these benefits, if done correctly, public relations can decrease the amount of negative press about your company. This article will cover all about benefit from public relations in my company.

How PR can help your company

There are many reasons that it's a good idea for most businesses to work hard on their public relations, and you're probably starting to see why. You must consider these points and use them as guidance when working to improve your public relations. If you don't do this, then it will be tough for your business to succeed in the long run.

What purpose does PR serve?

PR is designed for several purposes, but the most common goals are to:

a. Keep the public informed. Many people desire to know and understand their communities or companies, which PR can help with by letting them know about and understand local issues, history, and culture, as well as significant events in the community that they may have otherwise not known about.

b. Promote ideas or goods. PR can help promote ideas and goods that are not easily seen. For example, if a company from the county is looking to expand in another country area, PR can help get the word out about their products or services by letting people know what they offer.

c. Create loyal customers who are willing to spend more money than other companies in your industry. It could be done through coupons, advertisements or even concerts thrown for customers and friends of the company to buy more products.

Public relations is one of those skills that many people seem to think they don't need but by no means are those the only benefits of PR. Effective public relations can help a company in so many ways, and this blog post will help you realize the true worth of PR.

Build more relationships with customers

The first and most crucial way public relations can help your company is by building more relationships with customers. As a business owner, you want to create strong relationships with customers so that they will continue to buy from you and not from one of your competitors. You must always look for opportunities to cross-sell or up-sell. You might also want to look for opportunities in which you can support your customer or give them something extra like a gift or some other sort of surprise.

Increase trust in your company

Public relations can help your company is by increasing the trust between your company and the public. One of the

most important things you need to do as a business owner is to be honest, and trustworthy. You need to have a reputation for being honest and reliable because when people come to you for something, whether it's for advice or a new product, they will be more likely to buy from you if they believe that you are trustworthy.

The first step in having a solid reputation for being trustworthy is by being honest. It's okay to tell the truth even if you don't like what people say about you. Believe it or not, your customers appreciate it when you dare to admit when you are in the wrong and stand behind your company. If you confess that you're wrong about anything and acknowledge that you screwed up, people will respect that more than if they thought it was okay to lie their way out of things.

Get the word out about your company

Public relations can benefit your company is by getting the word out about your company. When you have good public relations tactics in place, you will be able to get your company recognized for the great things that you are doing. You will also get your customers talking about what a great company you are, and that's an effective way to spread the word about what you can offer them.

It is one of the most powerful benefits of public relations. Once you have an excellent reputation with your customers, they will be more likely to recommend you to other people. They won't necessarily do this for free, but it's a lot less expensive than advertising on television or any other form of traditional media.

Reduce negative press

The most important way that public relations can help your company is by reducing the amount of negative press about your company. People are more likely to share their stories when they have a terrible experience with a business than when they have a positive one. For example, suppose you go online and search for reviews of some restaurants in your area. In that case, you will probably find many more bad reviews about a chain restaurant than you will about an independent restaurant.

The independent restaurant has a smaller chance of having someone who had a terrible experience with them. Still, the chain restaurant will have thousands of people with bad experiences. In this case, you will not only find that chain restaurants have a more negative press, but you will also notice that some of those stories are filled with lies.

The most important thing for businesses to do is to make an effort to solve every problem that comes their way and always be willing to take responsibility for their mistakes. If you are going to be able to take responsibility for your mistakes and solve problems, you need to make sure that you're practicing good public relations.

Increase awareness for your company

Public relations can help your company is by increasing awareness of your company. You want to make sure that people know

who you are and what you're all about, and this is one of the best ways to do it. It's tough to gain a lot of attention for your business, but it will become much easier if you have the right public relations tactics.

Lower the volume of negative press

It can help a company is by lowering the volume of negative press about your company. Sometimes when you're the primary source of bad press for a company, it can be challenging for them to move forward. It can affect your customers, employees, and even your reputation. It's essential to keep an eye out for any negative stories about you so that you can work to improve them.

Reduce complaints

Public relations can help the company is by reducing the number of complaints about your company. Customers and other people who have had negative experiences with your company are more likely to share those stories with the public if they can put their dissatisfaction into words. If a business can work hard enough, these complaints will disappear over time because customers won't continue to tell the same story repeatedly.

Increase referrals from happy customers

The eighth way they can help your business is by increasing the number of referrals from your customers. The more that your customers are satisfied, the more likely it will be that they will share their experience with the word. Some people will specifically recommend your company to everyone they know. Even if your customers don't go around telling people about how great you are, it's still a good idea for businesses to practice good public relations tactics.

Improve your online reputation

Public relations can help a business by improving your business's online reputation. If your company has an excellent online reputation and is working hard to keep it that way, you shouldn't have to worry too much about negative reviews. The more positive press that you have out there, the less likely it is that anyone will be willing to share their negative experience with the world. If someone tries to make their complaints heard, they won't be able to do anything about it because they will look like the bad guy.

Improve your general reputation

The tenth way public relations can help your business is by improving your general reputation. You want to take things in your life seriously, and this should include your company. You never know who will end up talking about you or what they might say. If you have a terrible reputation, people will not only be less likely to support your company; they will be more likely to harass you.

7 tips for improving PR

Public relations is an integral part of everyday life. It helps companies, communities, and individuals in their efforts to connect. It can be used to get the word out about new products and services, let ethical problems be known, and show others how good of a job someone has done. Public relations also

does not just have one goal but many goals because it is designed for diverse purposes such as promoting a product or service, expressing an idea or ideology, or managing media attention after some event such as a natural disaster. PR is a vast topic encompassing many other issues discussed in the media, politics, and business. here is how you can expand your public relations:

1. Create a PR plan

Everyone wants to be successful, yet no one knows how to do it. A plan is an excellent way to succeed in public relations and help you reach your goals. Having a project to follow can make writing press releases and articles much more accessible than if you were trying to figure out what you will write and how you will present it.

2. Set and meet deadlines

Press releases and articles that do not reach their deadlines for publication can be very damaging. It has been proven that the more time a press release takes to get its reader, the less effective it is because the reader may have already moved on to something else. Press releases are usually sent through email to a news outlet's public relations department, so they will get lost if they are not published as soon as they come in. To ensure that your press release gets posted on time, set up a deadline and keep track of its due date.

3. Get experience

The best way to get experience with public relations is to work for a company or organization that has public relations as part of their everyday duties or in a college or university PR department. Working for a company can help you learn about how a company uses PR, how to talk about the company's goals and how to interact with members of the press corps. Working in an organization can allow you to speak to different people, practice writing press releases and articles, and learn how to give interviews.

4. Join a PR club or organization

When working in public relations clubs and organizations, you will be able to network with other students working at companies, organizations, or media outlets. You can also get experience by writing articles for their newsletter and by helping them with their PR projects, such as getting press releases published on the web.

5. Get involved in something that requires public relations skills

If you are interested in a subject commonly covered by the media, it will be challenging to practice your PR skills until you get involved in something. The more you apply yourself with a passion for public relations, the more you will become accustomed to putting out information that people need to know.

6. Understand what makes people tick

The art of gaining knowledge of people is known as psychographics. Knowing what makes people tick allows you to develop strategies that speak to a particular audience. If you are an employee trying to get information about a product out to the public, you will have more success if you know what your audience needs and how that product can be used to decrease their problems.

7. Use PR technology

Many forms of technology can be used in public relations, such as the Internet, email, radio, and television. Businesses commonly use technology as a form of advertising because it is cheaper than traditional forms of advertising.

Why is PR so Important to My Business?

Public relations is one of the most important aspects of any business. But why is Public Relations so important to my business? Just look at the top corporations, banks, and multi-national businesses—you'll see that they all have a PR department. Public relations help create a strong brand for your business, which gives you an edge over your competitors.

A strong brand can help draw in customers and build your reputation. You'll also be able to communicate with the media. Public relations is the art of managing the flow of information about a company or group to influence its public image positively. They play a fundamental role at every level of business and industry, from small start-ups to established corporations.

Public relations are also one of the most cost-effective methods of communication. It is also a lot easier to implement than other strategies that require a lot of manpower, like advertising. It is the practice of managing the messages about your company or organization to promote a favorable public image, protect its interests, and respond to inquiries. Public relations can be a challenge for any company of any size.

14 reasons why PR is important

Public Relations is much important for so any business to grow and scale. If you're a start-up with only a few employees, for instance, PR is often the best choice because it's not as expensive as advertising and can be done by a single individual. Now lets get on the reasons and advantages of public relations in businesses.

1. PR helps make you attractive

Whether done in-house or by a PR agency, publicity helps increase your brand's awareness, reputation, and visibility to the public as well as to potential customers. All three of these components are key to successful marketing. Public Relations helps communicate your message directly to the public and create awareness about your business in local, regional, and national news outlets, both online and in print.

Having a brand name may seem like a given, but it is not for many companies. Various aspects play into the success of a brand; your logo, tagline, and even your product packaging. PR is key to making sure your brand name sticks in the minds of consumers. Public Relations is the most important facet of a company's marketing mix.

2. PR helps you get the word out

Once your product, service, or company has become known by consumers and potential customers, public relations has the challenge of getting it out there. The traditional advertising method is the most cost-effective form of marketing, but it's often not the most effective. News media is the most common way to get your product or service in front of your target audience, but social media sites like Facebook and Twitter are also used.

Social media is a great way to connect with potential customers, recruit staff and build brand awareness. Many companies have a dedicated PR position to reach out to social media sites, but it is a personal challenge for many business owners. There are key players to hit and content to create, so that PR can be a time-consuming process.

3. PRs is a marketing tool

PR also plays a role in managing your brand's image and image perception, essential in the long term. According to a report by CBIZ Human Resources Solutions, companies that are most successful at public relations are 18% more likely to see growth in their bottom line.

This is where online PR comes in. Online public relations allows you to maintain control of your brand's message, and it can also allow you to respond to inquiries more quickly. Crisis management is another aspect of public relations. When your brand is under attack or your business is faltering, you need a plan in action immediately.

4. PR builds your business

There are many ways that PR can help grow your business and attract new customers, including any aspect of public relations such as blogging, web design, and social networking. Social media, in particular, gives potential customers a platform in which they can connect with your company.

It's often a good idea to put as much effort into your web design as you do your PR. Your online live website presence will be the first impression an audience has of your company, so ensure it's professional and informative. Market research on social media is a great way to determine which platforms are the most effective and allocate time accordingly.

5. PR makes you memorable

The data we have on our brains is tremendous, but there is only little we remember with time. To be memorable, you need to continue to reach the public multiple times. You may have a way of reaching their attention now, but if they are not satisfied with your product or service, they will not remember you.

This is where PR can step in. The purpose is to make a picture that stands out and sticks in the minds of consumers so that they will remember your company or product. If someone is thinking about buying something, many different factors go into their final decision. If another brand or product comes up after they've decided on yours, it's likely your PR will come to mind, and you'll get the sale.

6. Develop your corporate image

It is not enough to provide excellent service to your customers. You must also create an image for your company to attract other customers and build brand awareness among consumers. Public relations is a critical part of marketing your company and can bring in new business by increasing brand awareness and credibility.

Your reputation will play a role in the way your business operates. If you build a reputation for being honest and sharing details, you will be rewarded with more customers.

7. PR helps you find the right message.

This is why it's important to continually monitor what consumers and the public say about your product or service. Your message will live or die by what is said. It is important to listen to what the public says and share that with your customers. That information will help you craft the right message for your company.

You may need to change or adjust some of your PR efforts as your brand develops, but monitoring how consumers are talking about you will be important. If you're a traditional business and don't have the means to do this, PR is a great way to find out what your potential customers know about your product.

8. Improve your credibility

Have you got interested in making a good impression on investors? Do it by doing some good PR, such as updating your LinkedIn profile, if you don't already have one. Also, ensure your business contact information is correct. This can be done by updating your profiles on numerous social media sites.

You may also consider building a LinkedIn group or following industry-related people. If they follow you back, they are more likely to view your company as credible. There are all kinds of ways that public relations can help you improve your credibility and that of your company.

9. PR builds your reputation

One of the best ways PR can help your company is by building its reputation. There are many ways to do this, ranging from customer testimonials to positive press at industry events. Public relations are critical in business, and PR professionals across the country are always torn on how to best optimize their media. They want to ensure that they provide a good look for their brands while also gaining new customers.

It's not just the press that makes a difference. Word of mouth can be just as powerful. If you have happy and satisfied customers, they're going to tell their friends. This is one of the most effective ways to build a good reputation for your company. Any publicity can make a reputation for your company and your products.

10. PR helps you think outside the box

Public relations is good for getting your ideas in front of the public. You can spread the word about a new product and let customers decide whether to buy it. This technique is often used by businesses developing a product for the first time. It provides facts about potential consumers to gauge demand before making expensive products. You can easily hear how people feel about your product and then take it there.

11. PR is more cost-effective than advertising

Although advertising can be more expensive, successful public relations campaigns will help you save money in the long term. It's as there are so many aspects of public relations that you don't pay for, such as your product's logo and tagline.

Each part of advertising has a price, but with PR, you spend only on PR to drive brand awareness and sales if you plan.

12. PR is the first step in branding

It's essential to begin thinking about branding your company when you launch a new product or service, not just through advertising. Good PR campaigns will help you build your brand image, so it's important to get that started as soon as possible. This can be done through a campaign, such as a 24-hour launch party, designed to get the word out about your product and create goodwill with customers.

It's the perfect way to kick off your branding campaign. Public relations can also help you market your products and services once, if not several times. If you build a good message and drive good product reviews, your company will experience a rise in brand awareness and sales.

13. PR keeps your customers happy

It is particularly true when you sell your products or services that are illegal, unstable, or dangerous, such as firearms and drugs. If new laws are passed, your best bet is to stay ahead of the curve and be proactive in public relations. This is why it's important to keep the public up-to-date on new laws and potential regulatory changes. The government tends to react to consumer demands regarding areas people are concerned, such as health care, consumer safety, and security.

It's your job to share your customers' concerns with the public. By doing this, you can make sure your company complies with new laws and regulations that may affect your business. It's also an opportunity to improve relationships with customers and potential customers. Social media can help you do this by staying on top of the news and responding to customers' concerns before they become a problem.

14. PR takes the pressure off you

Your employees will make a huge difference in how well your PR campaign goes, but if you're up to the challenge, it's up to you to plan and execute this campaign. If you're seeking a new job, many hiring professionals want to know what kind of experience you have with public relations.

You need to show that you can communicate effectively and clearly, which is the key to a successful PR campaign. PR will help you learn how to manage people and even set the stage for making important connections in the future. So, despite the hard work in a successful public relations campaign, you will see results.

Final thoughts

Public relations can help you sell more products or services, keep customers happy and make your company more valuable. Public relations basics learning and implementation are easy, so get them into your business. Public relations is a great way to grow your business and reach out to potential clients and customers.

You can see that public relations are a long-term investment rather than one you make every day, but it will eventually pay off. A PR campaign will bring a long-term increase in the sales of your products. This increase means that you'll see better profits over time and that your company can survive for a long time.

Advertisers

This is the start of taking your business to the

NEXT LEVEL

Transform your business

Prepare to grow and scale

Optimize your work flow

Transform your business

SAB
WHERE RESULTS MATTER

strategicadvisorboard.com